E. Nesbit's
The Railway Children

Written by E. Nesbit
Adapted by Annie Dalton
Illustrated by Maxim Larin

Published by Pearson Education Limited, Edinburgh Gate, Harlow, Essex, CM20 2JE.

www.pearsonschools.co.uk

Text © Annie Dalton 2013
Original illustrations © Pearson Education Limited 2013
Illustrated by Maxim Larin, Advocate Art
Designed by Vincent Shaw-Morton

The right of Annie Dalton to be identified as author of this work has been asserted by her in accordance with the Copyright, Designs and Patents Act 1988.

First published 2013

17 16 15 14 13
10 9 8 7 6 5 4 3 2 1

British Library Cataloguing in Publication Data
A catalogue record for this book is available from the British Library

ISBN 978 0 435 14409 8

Copyright notice
All rights reserved. No part of this publication may be reproduced in any form or by any means (including photocopying or storing it in any medium by electronic means and whether or not transiently or incidentally to some other use of this publication) without the written permission of the copyright owner, except in accordance with the provisions of the Copyright, Designs and Patents Act 1988 or under the terms of a licence issued by the Copyright Licensing Agency, Saffron House, 6–10 Kirby Street, London EC1N 8TS (www.cla.co.uk.) Applications for the copyright owner's written permission should be addressed to the publisher.

Printed and bound in the UK by Ashford Colour Press.

Acknowledgements
We would like to thank Bangor Central Integrated Primary School, Northern Ireland; Bishop Henderson Church of England Primary School, Somerset; Bletchingdon Parochial Church of England Primary School, Oxfordshire; Brookside Community Primary School, Somerset; Bude Park Primary School, Hull; Carisbrooke Church of England Primary School, Isle of Wight; Cheddington Combined School, Buckinghamshire; Dair House Independent School, Buckinghamshire; Deal Parochial School, Kent; Glebe Infant School, Gloucestershire; Henley Green Primary School, Coventry; Lovelace Primary School, Surrey; Our Lady of Peace Junior School, Slough; Tackley Church of England Primary School, Oxfordshire; and Twyford Church of England School, Buckinghamshire for their invaluable help in the development and trialling of the Bug Club resources.

Every effort has been made to contact copyright holders of material reproduced in this book. Any omissions will be rectified in subsequent printings if notice is given to the publishers.

Contents

Chapter 1
Two Visitors   5
Chapter 2
Apple Pie for Breakfast   16
Chapter 3
The Kind Old Gentleman   26
Chapter 4
Bobbie's Birthday   35
Chapter 5
Prisoners and Captives   42
Chapter 6
Landslide!   52
Chapter 7
Heroes   62
Chapter 8
The Pride of Perks   70
Chapter 9
The Terrible Secret   82
Chapter 10
The Hound in the Red Jersey   90
Chapter 11
Bobbie Meets the Train   100

CHAPTER ONE
Two Visitors

They were not railway children to begin with. They were just three ordinary children who lived with their father and mother in the Red House – an ordinary red-brick house with coloured glass in the front door.

The eldest was Bobbie, which was short for Roberta.

Next came Peter; he planned to be an engineer when he grew up.

The youngest was Phyllis, who tended to break things.

Their mother was different to other children's mothers. For one thing she was always writing stories. She also made up funny poems for special occasions, like the arrival of the new kitten or the time they all caught the mumps.

Their father was just perfect: never cross and wonderful at mending things when no one else could.

The children had everything they needed to be happy: good clothes, a nursery full of toys, a cheerful nursemaid. They were happy, but they didn't know how happy until their old life at the Red House was over forever.

The change came suddenly and without any warning.

The family were having supper when Ruth, their maid, came in looking flustered.

"Two gentlemen have come to see you, Sir," she said to Father. "I've shown them into the library."

"They probably want money for the church funds," said Mother with a sigh. "Do get rid of them quickly. It's almost the children's bedtime."

But for some reason the two gentlemen

didn't seem to want to leave.

Mother tried to make the time pass, by telling the children a story about a green-eyed princess, but raised voices from the library made it hard to listen. Bobbie thought their father's voice sounded different to the voice he normally used when people came to see him about church funds.

Everybody breathed a sigh of relief when the library bell rang at last.

"They're going!" said Phyllis. "He's rung to have them shown out."

But instead of showing anybody out, Ruth came in, looking more flustered than ever.

"The Master wants you to step into the study, mum," she said. "He looks like the dead. I think it's bad news. Perhaps it's a death or a bank has gone bust or —"

"That'll do, Ruth," Mother told her, and she hurried to the library.

There was more talking but the children couldn't hear what was being said.

The bell rang again and Ruth fetched a cab. They heard boots tramp through the hall and down the steps. The cab drove away and the front door shut. Mother came back in. Her face was as white as her lace collar and her eyes looked very big and shining. Her mouth was just a line of pale red, not its proper shape at all.

"It's bedtime," she said. "Ruth will put you to bed."

"But you promised we could stay up because Father's come home," said Phyllis.

"Father's been called away on business," said Mother. "Please, darlings, just go to bed."

Phyllis and Peter obeyed, but Bobbie hung back. "It wasn't bad news, was it?" she whispered. "Is anyone dead – or …"

"Nobody's dead," said Mother and she almost pushed Roberta away. "I can't tell you anything tonight, my pet. Just go, dear. Go *now*."

Later, Mother came up and kissed all three children as they lay sleeping. Bobbie was the only one who was awake. In the dark, she heard the catching of her mother's breath but she lay mousey-still and said nothing.

"If Mother doesn't want us to know she's been crying," she said to herself, "we *won't* know it, that's all."

When the children came downstairs the next morning, Mother had already gone out.

"To London," Ruth said, and left them to their breakfast.

The children came home for their dinner at one, but Mother wasn't there. She still wasn't there at tea time.

It was nearly seven before she came in, looking so ill and tired that the children felt they couldn't ask her any questions at all. She sank into an arm chair. Phyllis took the long pins out of her mother's hat, while Bobbie took off her gloves. Peter unfastened their mother's walking shoes and fetched her velvety house slippers.

When she had had a cup of tea, Mother said, "Now, my darlings, I want to tell you something. Those men last night brought very bad news and Father will be away for some time. I want you all to help me and not to make things any harder for me."

Bobbie held Mother's hand against her cheek. "We will," she promised.

"You can help me most by being good and not quarrelling when I'm away," Mother went on, "for I shall have to be away a great deal. I want you to promise not to ask me any questions about this trouble and not to ask anybody else any questions."

"Is it something to do with the Government?" asked Bobbie, for their father worked in a Government office.

"Yes," said Mother. "Now it's bedtime, my darlings. And don't worry. It will all come right in the end."

Upstairs, the girls carefully folded their clothes, the only way they could think to be good.

Phyllis sighed. "Remember how you used to say our life was so dull? Nothing ever happened like in books? Well, now something *has* happened."

"I never wanted to make Mother unhappy," said Bobbie. "Everything's perfectly horrible."

Life continued to be perfectly horrible for

weeks. It made it worse that the servants kept hinting that they knew what had happened to the children's father.

One day, Peter made a booby trap over the bathroom door and caught Ruth as she was passing through.

"You'll come to a bad end!" she shouted. "If you don't mend your ways, you'll go to the same place your precious father's gone!"

Bobbie repeated this to Mother and, next day, Ruth was sent away.

One morning, Mother came down to breakfast, very pale. She tried to smile as she said, "Now my pets, everything is settled. We're going to go to live in the country. Such a dear little house. I know you'll love it."

A whirling week of packing followed. Not just clothes, but chairs and tables, crockery, blankets, candlesticks, carpets, bedsteads and saucepans.

"Aren't you packing this?" Bobbie asked, pointing to a cabinet inlaid with turtle-shell and brass.

"We can't take everything," said Mother.

"We seem to be taking all the ugly things," said Bobbie.

"We're taking the useful ones," said Mother. "We've got to play at being poor for a bit, my darling."

At last all the ugly useful things had been packed up and were taken away in a van.

Next day a cab came to take them to the railway station: the start of their long journey to their new home in the country.

They enjoyed looking out of the train window at first but, as dusk began to fall, they soon grew sleepy.

At last they felt Mother shaking them gently, saying, "Wake up, dears. We're there."

They waited, shivering on the platform while their baggage was taken off. The train pulled out of the station puffing out clouds of steam, and the children watched the tail

lights of the guard's van disappear into the distant darkness.

They didn't know then how they would grow to love the railway, or how it would become the centre of their new life, or what changes and wonders it would bring. They only shivered and hoped it wasn't too far to the new house.

After a long, uphill walk along a dark country road, they reached their new home.

There was no light in any of the windows.

Everyone hammered at the door but no one came.

At last, Mother discovered the key under the doorstep and let them in.

Inside, Mother hunted around for a candle and lit it. By its pale glimmer the children saw a large, bare kitchen with a stone floor. There were no curtains, no hearth rug. The kitchen table from home stood in the middle of the room. The chairs were in one corner and the pots, brooms and crockery in another. The black grate just showed cold, dead ashes.

There was a sudden scampering, rustling

sound from inside the walls of the house.

"What's that?" cried the girls.

"Probably rats," said Peter, just as a sudden draught blew out the candle.

"I wish we hadn't come," said Phyllis, in the dark.

CHAPTER TWO
Apple Pie for Breakfast

Mother quickly relit the candle. "This is quite an adventure, isn't it?" she said brightly. "I suppose Mrs Viney has put our supper in the dining room. Let's go and see."

They took their one candle into the dining room which opened out of the kitchen. Unlike the kitchen, which was whitewashed, the dining room was dark wood from floor to ceiling. There was a table and chairs, the familiar breakfast-room furniture from their old home, but no supper.

They went from room to room, finding more of their old belongings from the Red

House, but there was nothing to eat.

"That old woman must have walked off with our money and not bought us any food," Mother exclaimed.

"Shan't we have any supper?" asked Phyllis, dismayed. She stepped back on to a soap dish, which cracked.

"Oh, yes," said Mother. "We just have to open one of those big packing cases. Phyllis, do mind where you're walking. Peter, please hold the light."

Peter held the candle while Mother tried to open the packing case. It was very securely nailed down but with the help of the kitchen poker she managed it at last.

"Hurray! Candles!" said Mother. "You girls can light them. There must be saucers somewhere in here."

So the girls lit candles. The head of the first match flew off and stuck to Phyllis's finger, but, as Bobbie said, it was only a *little* burn.

Then Bobbie fetched coal and wood and lit a fire.

The firelight and candlelight made the

dining room look very different. Now they could see that the dark walls were of wood, carved here and there into little wreaths.

"That's better!" said Mother, coming in with a tray. "I'll just get a tablecloth."

Everyone cheered up at the sight of their delightful and unusual supper. There were biscuits, sardines, raisins and candied peel and marmalade. To drink, they had ginger beer and water out of willow-patterned cups because the glasses couldn't be found.

When the meal was over, they quickly made up their beds.

"Good night, my chicks," said Mother. "I'm sure there aren't really any rats. But if a mouse comes, just scream and I'll come and tell it what I think of it." Then she went to her own room.

Early next morning, Bobbie woke Phyllis by pulling her hair gently but firmly.

"Wassermarrer?" asked Phyllis, not properly awake.

"We're in the new house, remember? No servants or anything. Let's creep downstairs and have everything beautiful before Mother gets up. Peter is getting dressed."

The children lit the fire, put the kettle on and set the table for breakfast. Then they went out again into the fresh, bright morning.

They found some stables and an outbuilding and, although the house seemed to stand all alone in a field of soft smooth turf, they saw where the garden had hidden itself, with a high wall all around.

It was hilly country. Down below they could see the line of the railway and the yawning mouth of a tunnel. The station itself was out of sight. Running across one end of the valley was a great bridge with tall arches.

"Let's go and look at the railway," suggested Peter. "There might be trains passing."

"We can see them from here," said Bobbie, yawning. "Let's sit down a bit."

The children all sat down on a large, flat grey stone.

When Mother came out to look for them at eight o'clock, she found them fast asleep in the morning sun.

They had set the kettle to boil at about half past five. By eight the fire had been out for some time, the water had all boiled away and the bottom was burned out of the kettle.

"It doesn't matter," said Mother, "because I've found another room."

In the confusion of the night before, they'd mistaken the door for a cupboard. It was a little square room and on its table was a joint of cold roast beef, with bread, butter, cheese and an apple pie.

"Apple pie for breakfast!" said Peter with a grin.

"This is the supper we should have had last night," said Mother, smiling. "I found a note from Mrs Viney. She's coming this morning at ten."

The day passed in helping to unpack all their belongings. Soon their legs were aching from running around carrying clothes and china and from putting everything into its proper place.

It was not until quite late in the day that Mother said, "That'll do for now! I'll lie down for an hour so as to be fresh as a daisy by supper-time."

The children looked at each other. Each of them had the same thought. The railway!

So to the railway they went. It was all downhill over smooth short turf. Here and there, grey and yellow rocks stuck out like candied peel from the top of a cake.

The way ended in a steep run and a wooden fence – and there was the railway with the shining metals and the telegraph wires and signals.

They all climbed onto the top of the fence. Suddenly there was a rumbling sound and, next minute, a train had rushed out of the tunnel with a shriek and a snort. They felt the rush of its passing and the pebbles on the line jumped and rattled as it went by.

"I wonder if that train was going to London," Bobbie said. "London's where Father is."

"Let's go down to the station and find out," said Peter.

They walked along the edge of the line with the telegraph wires humming over their heads until they eventually reached the railway station.

It was exciting to arrive at the station, not through the booking office, but by the sloping end of the platform. There were a great many crossing lines at the station. Some of them just ran into a yard and stopped short. Trucks stood on the rails here and on one side was a great heap of coal. They peeped into the porters' room and saw one porter half asleep behind his newspaper.

As they were leaving, a gong sounded over the station door and the porter sleepily emerged. The children said politely, "How do you do?", then they set off back to the Three Chimneys, the house that was now their home.

As the weeks passed, the children's memories of their old life in the Red House grew to seem like a dream. They got used to being without Father, though they did not forget him. They got used to not going to school and they got used to seeing very little of Mother, who now spent almost all day shut up in her upstairs room writing. At tea time she came downstairs and read aloud the stories she had written.

Then in June came three wet days. The rain came down straight as lances and it was very cold. They all went up to Mother's room and knocked on the door.

"What is it?" said Mother's voice.

"May I light a fire?" said Bobbie. "We're so cold."

"No, darlings, we can't afford to light fires in June," said Mother cheerfully. "Go and run around in the attic. That'll warm you up. Now run away, dears. I'm madly busy."

The children ran up to the attic and played at being bandits and by the time they came down for tea they were flushed and happy.

But when Phyllis went to a[sk for] bread and butter, Mother said, "[...] dear, not jam *and* butter. We ca[n't afford that] kind of luxury now."

Nobody spoke. Phyllis silently ate her slice of bread and butter followed by a slice of bread and jam.

Mother had *tried* to tell them, Bobbie thought, but they hadn't believed her. They'd just thought it was the kind of thing that grown-ups said. But now Bobbie had to face the awful truth. Without Father to take care of them, they were poor, and there was nothing they could do about it.

CHAPTER THREE
The Kind Old Gentleman

The children's feet had begun to wear a track in the grass between the Three Chimneys and the railway embankment. They couldn't seem to keep away. The railway felt like their only remaining link with their old lives. Soon they knew what times certain trains would be passing. The London train, they called the Green Dragon. They loved this train best of all because London was where Father was.

"If it were really a dragon we could stop it and ask it to take our love to Father," said Phyllis one morning, when they were waiting for the London train to come rushing out of the tunnel. "Let's all wave as it goes by," she suggested. "If it is a magic dragon, it will understand and take our love to him."

So when the Green Dragon came roaring out of the tunnel, all three children stood on the railing and waved. To their delight, an old gentleman waved back from a first class carriage. After that it became their routine to wave to the old gentleman every morning. The children liked to think that he was a friend of Father's. They imagined him cheerily reporting back how his children faithfully appeared to wave their love to their much-missed father, every day, rain or shine.

All this time, Mother was busy with her writing. When she finished a story she posted it off in a long blue envelope. Sometimes the stories came straight back and the children felt sorry for her. Other times she would wave a letter in the air and say, "He's taken my story, hurray! We can have buns for tea!"

But Mother must have been working too hard, because one day she had to stay in bed. Her head ached, her hands were burning hot and her throat was very sore. By evening she was so much worse that she asked Peter to go and fetch the doctor.

Dr Forrest came at once and said Mother had influenza. "I'll send down some medicine," he told them on the way out. "Make sure you light a fire to keep her warm." Then he gave them a list of special foods that Mother needed if she was to get better: grapes, soda water and beef tea.

Mother laughed when she saw it. "I can't afford all that!"

Bobbie went downstairs and told the others what Mother had said. "And there's no one but us to look after her and all we've got is a shilling," she finished.

"We can't buy all those things on the list with a shilling," said Phyllis.

"I know," said Bobbie, frowning. "We must think of another way."

After a while Phyllis said, "I might know *one* way …"

Later, when Bobbie had gone up to sit with Mother, Phyllis and Peter took a sheet out of the linen cupboard and got busy with a paint brush and a pot of blacking that Mrs Viney used to clean the grate.

Next morning, the doctor came. "Is everything all right?" he asked Bobbie. "I don't see any grapes or any beef tea."

"No, but you will tomorrow," said Bobbie firmly.

That morning, when the 9.15 train came out of the tunnel, the old gentleman in the first class carriage put down his newspaper to wave to the children as usual. But this morning there was only Peter and he was pointing at a white sheet nailed against the fence. On the sheet black-painted letters said:

LOOK OUT AT THE STATION

But when the old gentleman looked out, he just saw the flowers in the little station garden. It was only as the train was moving off again that he saw Phyllis dashing along the platform. "We've written you a letter!" she panted. She threw it into his hand as the train pulled out of the station.

The old gentleman opened his letter. This is what he read.

Dear Mr we do not know your name.

Mother is ill and the doctor says to give her the things at the end of the letter but she can't afford it. We do not know anybody here but you, because Father is away and we do not know the address. Father will pay you, or if he has lost all his money, Peter will pay you when he is a man. We promise it on our honour. Will you give the parcel to the Station Master, because of us not knowing what train you come down by?

Roberta, Phyllis, Peter

Underneath was the doctor's list. The old gentleman read it through twice and smiled to himself. Then he put it in his pocket and went on reading *The Times*.

That evening, there was a knock at the back door. The children rushed to open it, and there stood the station porter. He dumped down a big hamper on the flagstones. "Old gent," he said. "He asked me to fetch this up to you straight away."

"Thank you very much," said Peter, then he added, "I'm awfully sorry I haven't got two pence to tip you like Father does."

"I wasn't thinking about any tips!" said the porter, offended. "I only wanted to say I'm sorry your Mamma isn't so well." And he produced a bunch of flowers from his hat. "Just like a conjurer," Phyllis said afterwards.

Inside the hamper were all the things they had asked for and more, including peaches, two chickens, a bouquet of red roses and a bottle of lavender water. There was a letter inside too.

Dear Roberta and Phyllis and Peter

Your mother will want to know where these things came from. Tell her they were sent by a friend who heard she was ill. When she is well again, you must tell her all about it. And if she says you ought not to have asked for the things, tell her that I say you were quite right and I hope she will forgive me for taking the liberty of allowing myself a great pleasure.

The letter was signed G.P. something that the children couldn't read.

"I think we *were* right," said Phyllis.

"Of course we were right," said Bobbie.

"All the same," said Peter. "I don't look forward to telling Mother."

"We won't tell her until she's well," said Bobbie. "And then we shall be so happy we won't *care* if she's cross!"

A fortnight later the old gentleman looked out of his carriage to wave to the children as usual and saw them holding up another sheet bearing a new message.

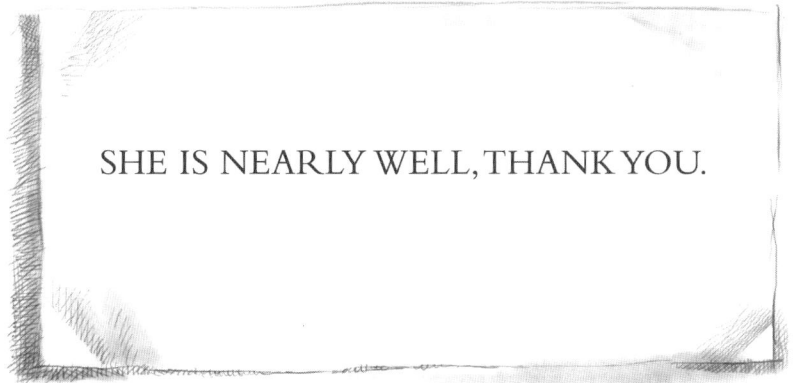

SHE IS NEARLY WELL, THANK YOU.

CHAPTER FOUR
Bobbie's Birthday

Once Mother was well again, the children knew they had to tell her where they had got all the wonderful things that had helped to make her better.

When they'd finished telling her, Mother was angrier than they had ever known her. That was horrible enough, but it was much worse when she began to cry. The children felt so dreadful that they cried, too. Then Mother dried her eyes and said, "I'm sorry I was so angry, darlings. Now listen. It's true that we're poor, but we have enough to live on. You mustn't go telling everyone our business. And you must never *ever* ask strangers to give you things."

They hugged her and promised that they never would.

"I'll write a letter to your old gentleman thanking him for his kindness," she said, "and we won't say any more about it."

The children took the letter down to the station and had an enjoyable talk with the porter who was fast becoming a friend. They learned that his name was Perks, that he was married with three children and that the lamps in front of the engines were called headlights and the ones at the back tail lights. "Which just shows", said Phyllis later, "that trains really *are* dragons in disguise, with proper heads and tails."

Next day was Bobbie's birthday. In the afternoon she was politely told to keep out of the way until tea time.

Bobbie went out into the garden. She knew everyone meant to be kind, but she did not want to spend her birthday afternoon all by herself. Now that she was alone, she had time to think, and one of the things she thought of was what Mother had said one of those feverish nights when her hands were so hot and her eyes so bright.

The words were: "Oh, what a big doctor's bill I'll have to pay."

Suddenly Bobbie made up her mind. Going out through the side door of the garden she walked until she came to the bridge that crossed the canal and there she waited in the sunshine, looking down at the water.

Presently there was a sound of wheels, just as she had hoped. The wheels were the wheels of the doctor's dogcart and in the cart was the doctor. When he saw her he pulled up and called out, "Your mother's not worse?"

"No, but –"

"Then what's the trouble?" he said. "Come on, out with it."

"Mother said I wasn't to go telling everyone we're poor," Bobbie said anxiously. "But you're not everyone, are you?"

"Certainly not," said the doctor cheerfully.

"Well, Mrs Viney told me that her

doctoring only cost her two pence a week because she belonged to a club. And I don't want Mother to be worried about bills, so please can we be in your club, the same as Mrs Viney?"

The doctor promised that he would make it all right with their mother if he had to make a special brand-new club just for her. Bobbie knew that her mother would not approve of what she'd done. But for once Bobbie felt that she was the one who was right, and she felt happy and relieved as she hurried home.

Phyllis and Peter met her at the back door. They were unnaturally clean and neat and Phyllis had a red bow in her hair. There was just time for Bobbie to tie up her hair with a blue bow before a little bell rang.

The bell was the signal for Bobbie to go into the dining room. Suddenly shy, she opened the door and found herself in a world of light and flowers. The shutters were shut and there were twelve lighted candles on the table, one for each of Bobbie's years. At

Bobbie's place was a wreath of blue forget-me-nots and several little packages.

"Come and open your presents," said Mother cheerfully.

There was a green and red needle book that Phyllis had made herself in secret moments. There was a silver brooch of Mother's shaped like a buttercup which Bobbie had loved for years and never thought would belong to her. There were two blue glass vases from Mrs Viney. And there were three birthday cards.

Mother fitted the forget-me-not crown on Bobbie's head.

"Now look at the table," she said.

There was a cake with 'Dear Bobbie' on it in pink sweets, and buns and jam, and wild flowers scattered everywhere.

After tea they played games and, while they were playing, Bobbie's forget-me-not wreath fell lopsidedly over one of her ears and stayed there. Then, when it was nearly bedtime, Mother read them a story.

"You won't sit up late working, will you, Mother?" Bobbie said as they said goodnight.

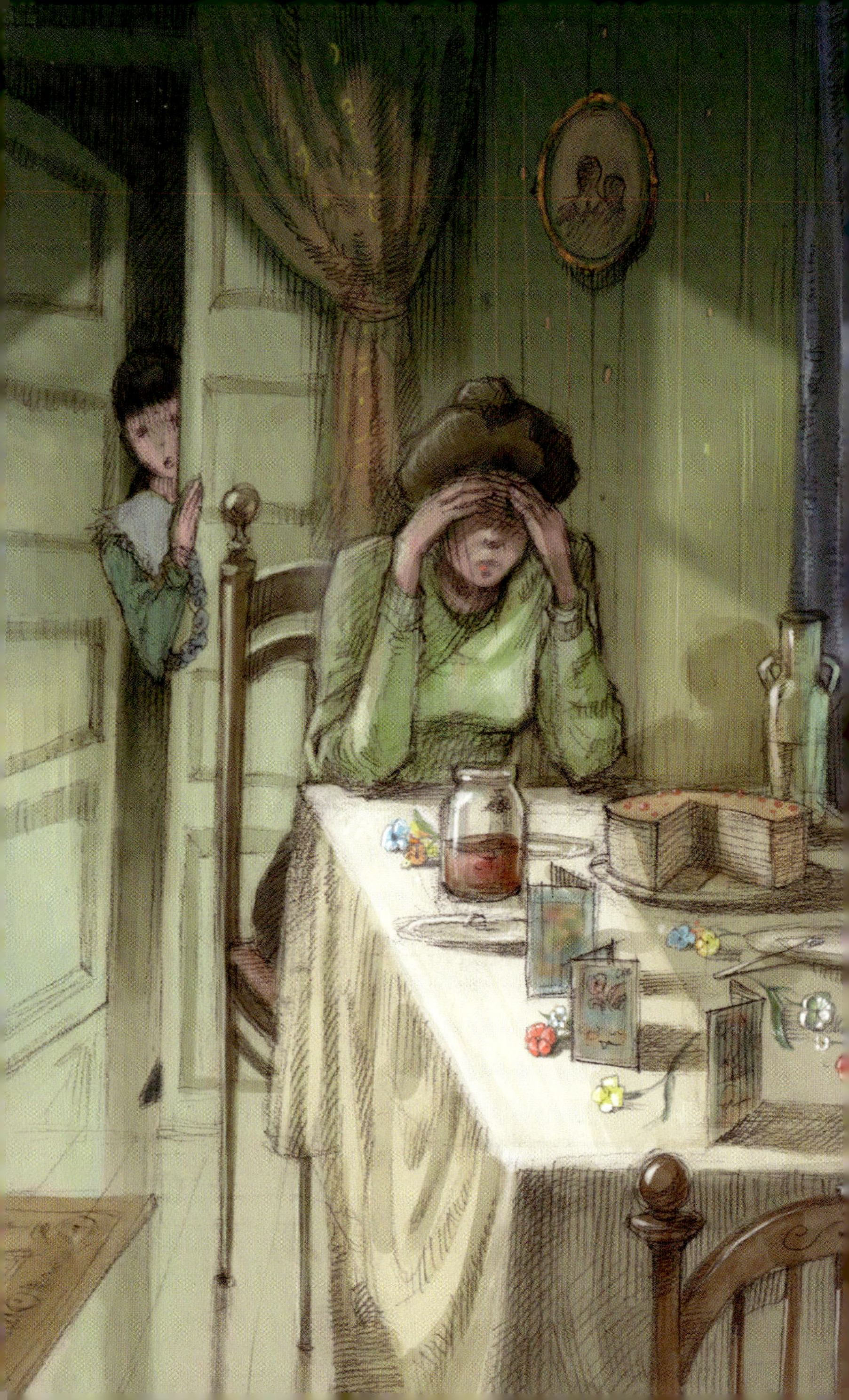

Mother promised she would just write to Father, then go to bed.

A few minutes later, Bobbie suddenly couldn't bear to be separated from her presents and crept back downstairs.

Mother was not writing. She was just sitting with her head in her hands.

Bobbie softly slipped away, saying to herself, "She doesn't want me to know she's unhappy, and I won't know. I *won't* know."

It made a sad end to her birthday.

CHAPTER FIVE
Prisoners and Captives

One day Mother had gone to Maidbridge to do some shopping. The children went to meet her off her train. When they arrived, they were surprised to see a small crowd gathering on the platform.

Everybody was talking at once.

"They should call the police," said a young man quickly.

"Take him to hospital, more like," said someone else.

They heard the firm voice of the station master. "I'll attend to this, *if* you please."

Then they heard a new voice that thrilled

the children through and through, for it spoke in a foreign language, a language they had never heard.

"What is it that he's saying?" asked a red-faced farmer.

"Sounds very much like French to me," said the station master.

"It isn't French," said Peter. "I don't know what it is. But it isn't French, I know that."

Now he could see the man who was causing all this excitement, an ill-looking man with long hair, wearing shabby clothes in a style Peter had never seen before. The man was coughing and trembling as he spoke in that strange foreign tongue.

"No, it's not French," said Peter with great confidence.

"Try him with French then, since you know so much," said the farmer.

"Parlay voo Frongsay?" Peter began slowly and boldly.

Everyone backed away as the wild-eyed man sprang forwards, catching at Peter's hands, and pouring out a flood of foreign words at great speed.

"There! Now *that*'s French!" Peter told the crowd proudly.

"What did he say?"

"I don't know," Peter admitted sheepishly.

"Take him into your room," Bobbie whispered to the station master. "Mother can talk French. She'll be here by the next train from Maidbridge."

The station master went to take the arm of the stranger, but the man cowered back.

"He thinks you're going to lock him up," said Bobbie. "I know he does – look at his eyes!" And suddenly, looking at those wild, hunted eyes, Bobbie found herself speaking some French words. "*Ma mere parlez Francais. Nous* – what's the French for 'being kind'"?

"*Bong* is 'good'," said Phyllis.

"*Nous etre bong pour vous.*"

The man seemed to understand that Bobbie meant to be kind. He let her take his hand and gently lead him into the station master's room. Phyllis and Peter followed behind and the station master shut the door on the crowd.

"I ought to send for the police," said the station master, "travelling by train without a ticket. Doesn't even know where he wants to go."

Bobbie was horrified to see that the stranger was crying. She quickly passed him her handkerchief so that nobody saw.

"I'm sure he hasn't done anything like you're sent to prison for," said Peter.

"I'll give him the benefit of the doubt till your mamma comes," said the station master. "Though I should like to know what nation's got the credit of *him*, that I should."

Just as they stopped talking, the train from Maidbridge was signalled.

"I'll stay with him till you bring Mother," said Bobbie.

"You're not afraid, Missie, are you?" said the station master.

"Oh, no," said Bobbie. "You wouldn't hurt me, would you?" She smiled at the stranger and he smiled back, a queer, crooked smile.

Then the heavy rattling swish of the incoming train swept past and the station master and Peter and Phyllis went out to meet it. A moment later, they came back with Mother.

She immediately began speaking in French and the stranger replied. The children could see from their mother's expression that he was telling her things that made her sorry and indignant, all at once.

"It's all right," Mother told the station master at last. "He's a Russian. He's lost his ticket and I'm afraid he's rather ill. If you don't mind, I'll take him home with me." She smiled at the station master's doubtful expression. "This gentleman is a great man in his own country," she explained. "He's a writer. I've read some of his books."

She spoke again in French to the Russian and the children saw surprise and gratitude in his eyes.

He politely offered his arm to Mother. She took it, but anyone could see that she was helping him along, not him helping her.

Phyllis and Peter ran on ahead to light the fire in the sitting room and Bobbie went to fetch the doctor.

When Bobbie and the doctor reached the Three Chimneys, the Russian was sitting in the armchair that had been Father's, stretching his feet to the blaze of a bright wood fire.

"His cough is very bad," the doctor told them later. "He needs to go straight to bed, and let him have a fire at night."

"He can have my room," said Mother. "It's the only one with a fireplace."

After she had lit the fire the doctor helped the stranger to bed.

There was a big black trunk in Mother's room that none of the children had ever seen unlocked. Now she unlocked it and took some clothes out – men's clothes – and set them to air by the fire.

Bobbie came in with more wood for the fire and saw the open trunk filled with Father's clothes.

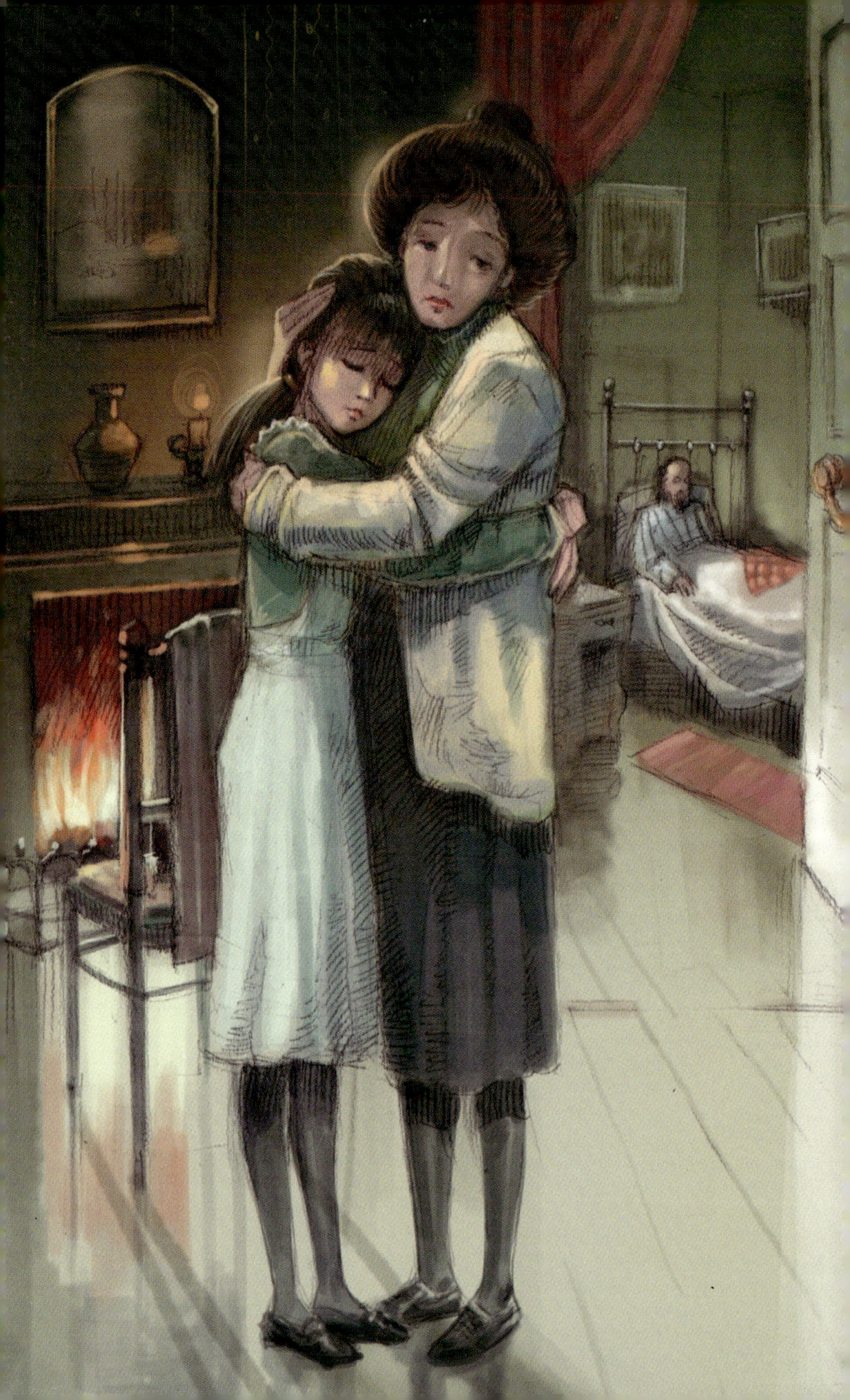

She quickly slipped from the room. Her heart was beating horribly. Why hadn't Father taken his clothes with him?

When Mother came out, Bobbie flung her arms around her waist. "Mother – Daddy isn't *dead*, is he?"

Her mother looked dismayed. "My darling, no! Daddy was quite well when I heard from him last, and he'll come back to us one day, I promise."

Later, Mother came into the girls' room. Peter followed her in, dragging his quilt.

"Now tell us what happened to the Russian gentleman," they begged Mother.

Their mother explained that when Russia was ruled by the Czar, it was forbidden to say anything about rich people doing wrong, or how to help poor people. If they did, they were sent to prison. "Our Russian visitor wrote a book about helping poor people," she said, "and he was sent to prison for it."

"But people only go to prison when they've done wrong," objected Peter.

"Or when judges *think* they've done

wrong," said Mother. "Yes, that's so in England, but in Russia it was different."

Mother described how the Russian was sent to Siberia to work in the mines alongside dangerous convicts. "Just for writing a good and noble book," Mother said. "Then the war came and he volunteered as a soldier, but he deserted the first chance he got."

"Wasn't that cowardly? To desert in a war?" asked Peter.

"Do you think he owed anything to a country that had done *that* to him?" said Mother. "Besides he was desperate to find out what had happened to his wife and children who had fled from Russia to England. As soon as he deserted, he came straight here to find them. He didn't have an address. All he knew was England. He thought he had to change at our station and then found he'd lost his wallet and his ticket. Oh, I do hope and pray he'll find his wife and children again!"

Phyllis was looking at her mother in surprise. "You seem very sorry for him, Mother," she said.

Their mother didn't answer for a while. Presently she said, "Dears, when you say your prayers, I think you might ask God to show His pity upon all prisoners and captives. Yes, all prisoners and captives," she repeated, swallowing.

CHAPTER SIX
Landslide!

In a few days their Russian guest was well enough to sit out in the garden. Now, instead of writing her stories, Mother was writing letters to MPs, trying to find out what had happened to his family.

The children wanted to show how friendly they felt to this man who had been sent to prison simply for writing about poor people, but if they just smiled at him all the time their smiles tended to get fixed like a hyena's. Then Bobbie reminded the others about the wild cherries. In the springtime they'd seen white cherry blossom blooming among the oaks and birches on the railway embankment, and now cherry time was finally here. The children agreed that cherries would make a perfect present.

Mother said they could take their lunch in a basket. "After you've finished your lunch you can fill the basket with cherries," she said with a smile.

When they reached the top of the cutting, the children leaned over the fence and looked down to where the railway lines lay at the bottom. Phyllis said the rocky sides of the cutting looked exactly like a mountain gorge. Among the rocks, seeds dropped by birds had taken root and grown into trees and bushes that overhung the cutting. Near the tunnel a flight of ladder-like wooden steps led down to the line.

They had almost reached the steps when Bobbie said, "What's that?"

They heard a rustling, whispering sound. As they listened, the noise stopped, then started again, but this time it was louder and more rumbling.

"Look!" Peter pointed at a tree.

It was moving – not the way trees move when the wind blows through them, but in one piece, as though it were alive and was marching down the side of the embankment.

"It's walking!" cried Phyllis, astonished.

"So are the others!" cried Bobbie. "It's like the woods in Macbeth."

"I always knew this railway was magic!" said Phyllis.

Now all the trees on the opposite bank seemed to be slowly walking down towards the railway line.

"This is *much* too magic for me," said Phyllis. "Let's go home."

Stones and loose earth were following the trees down the embankment and rattling on the railway lines far below.

"It's all coming down!" gasped Peter.

As he spoke, the enormous rock that had been holding up the trees slowly started to lean forwards.

Then rock and trees, grass and bushes came thundering down the embankment, falling on the line with a blundering crash.

A cloud of dust rose up.

Peter's face was white. "The 11.29 hasn't gone by yet. We must let them know at the station, or there'll be a terrible accident."

Bobbie started to run but Peter called her back.

"No time," he said. "The station's two miles away and it's already past eleven. I wish we had something red. We could run 'round the corner and wave it at the train."

Fright was making Phyllis red-faced and a bit damp.

"I wish I hadn't put on this stupid flannel petticoat. It's making me much too hot," she said.

"Phyllis, our petticoats are *red!*" said Bobbie. "Quick! Let's take them off!"

The girls hastily slipped off their petticoats. The children set off running, skirting the fallen heap of stones, rock, earth and crushed, uprooted trees. They reached the corner that hid the landslide from the straight line of track.

"Now!" said Peter, grabbing hold of Bobbie's petticoat.

"You're not going to tear them?" Phyllis said anxiously.

"He can tear them to little pieces if he likes," said Bobbie. "If we don't stop the train in time, people could die."

She took the red flannel petticoat back from Peter and tore it off an inch from the band. Then she tore the other in the very same way.

"There!" said Peter, tearing in his turn. He divided each petticoat into three pieces. "Now we've got six flags." He checked his watch. "And we've got seven minutes. We need sticks for the flags."

Peter's knife was too blunt to cut wood, so they had to break off young saplings, quickly stripping off the leaves.

"We must cut holes in the flags and run the sticks through the holes," said Peter. The knife was sharp enough to cut flannel with.

Two of the flags were set up in the loose stones beneath the sleepers of the down line.

Then Phyllis and Bobbie each took a flag and stood ready to wave it as soon as the train came.

"I shall wave the other two myself," said Peter, "because it was my idea."

It seemed like a very long time that they waited.

Bobbie started to feel sick with suspense. Nobody would see their silly flags. The train would go rushing past them, tearing around the corner, and go crashing into that awful mound. Everyone would be killed.

Her hands trembled so that she could hardly hold her flag. Then came the distant rumble and hum of the metals and a puff of white steam showed far away along the stretch of line.

"Wave like mad!" said Peter. "When it gets to that big furze bush, remember to step back but carry on waving! Don't stand *on* the line, Bobbie!"

The train came rattling along very fast.

"They just won't see us! It's all no good!" cried Bobbie.

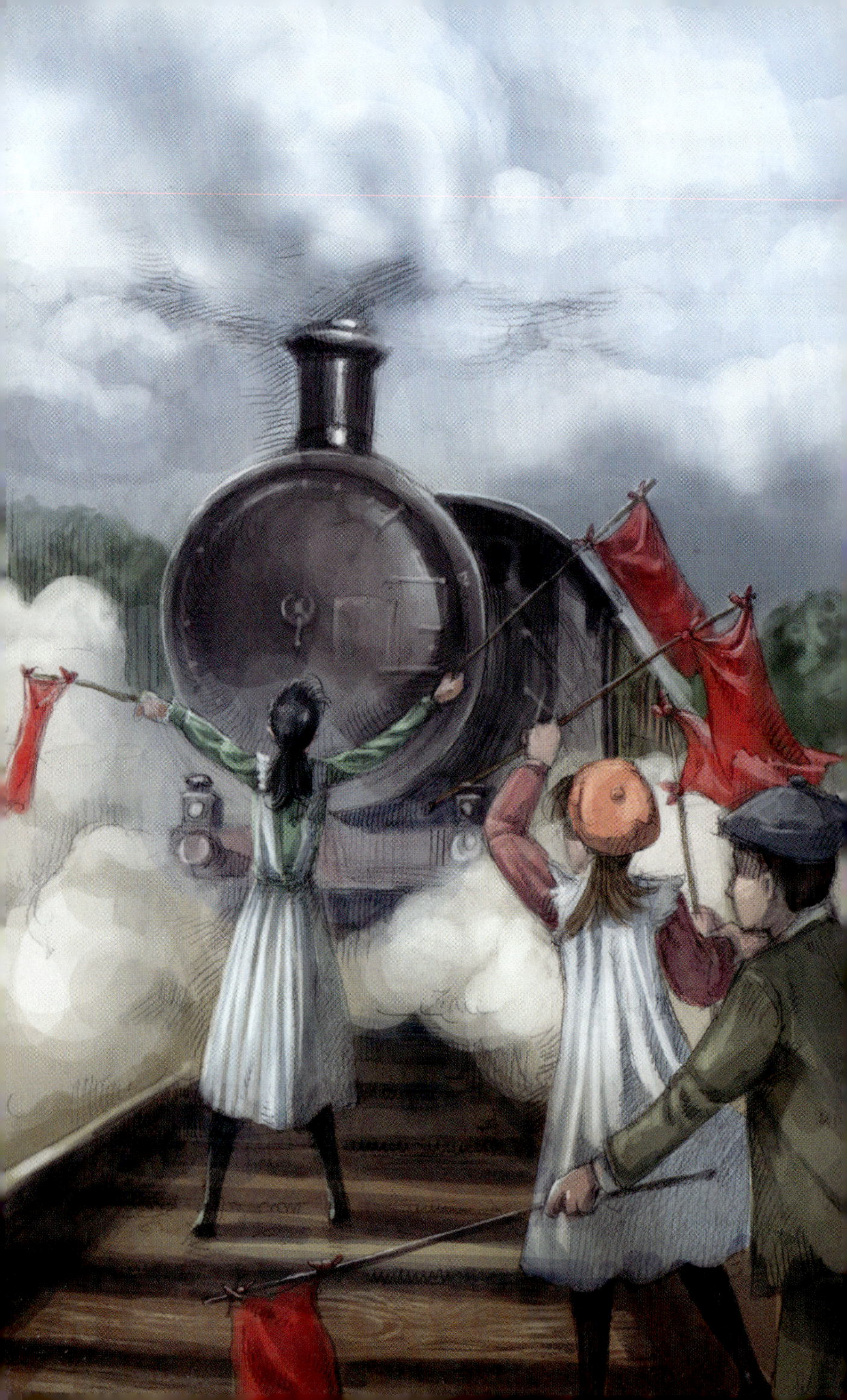

The two little flags on the line swayed as the approaching train shook and loosened the heaps of loose stones that held them up.

One of the flags slowly leaned over and fell on the line. Bobbie caught it up and waved it. Her hands didn't tremble now.

"Stand back!" Peter shouted suddenly and he dragged Phyllis back by the arm.

But Bobbie cried, "Not yet!" and went on waving her two flags right over the line.

The front of the engine looked black and enormous. Its voice was loud and harsh.

"Oh, stop, stop, *stop!*" But Bobbie's voice was lost in the oncoming rush of the train.

Afterwards she wondered whether the engine itself had heard her. It seemed as though it had, for it suddenly slackened its speed and stopped just a few metres from the place where Bobbie's two flags waved over the line.

The driver and the fireman jumped down from the engine. Peter and Phyllis ran to meet them and poured out their excited tale of the awful mound just around the corner.

The train had stopped yet Bobbie couldn't seem to stop waving her flags, though she did it increasingly feebly. When the others turned towards her she was lying motionless across the line, still gripping the sticks of her red flannel flags.

It was horrible to see Bobbie lying so white and quiet. She seemed to stay like this for a long time, until suddenly she sighed and opened her eyes and then began to cry.

Phyllis and Peter hadn't known what to do when Bobbie was fainting, but now that she was only crying they thumped her on the back and told her not to be silly, just as they always did.

"It was your prompt action saved the train and passengers," the station master told the children after the train had taken them back to the station. "You'll hear from the company about this."

As the children walked away, the train's passengers set up a cheer.

"Oh, listen," cried Phyllis. "That's for *us!*"

"And it was *us* that saved them!" said Peter.

Bobbie was still picturing the unsuspecting train rushing headlong towards the fallen rocks and earth. But she just said, "We never got any cherries after all."

CHAPTER SEVEN
Heroes

One morning a letter came addressed to Peter, Bobbie and Phyllis. The letter said that the railway company wished to give them an award for saving the train.

The children rushed to show Mother the letter. "You must wear your muslin dresses," she told the girls. "I want you to look your very best."

The day of the presentation ceremony came and the children went down to the station at the proper time.

The station master came out to meet

them in his best clothes and led them into the waiting room.

A carpet had been put down and there were pots of roses on the mantelpiece. Crowds of people had come for the ceremony: ladies in smart dresses and gentlemen in high hats. Best of all, their old gentleman was there. To their surprise, it turned out that he was a director of the railway.

He shook hands with the children.

Then a gentleman in spectacles, a superintendent of the railway, made a speech.

He said kind things about the children's bravery and, when he'd finished, everyone clapped and said, "Hear, hear!"

Next the old gentleman stood up and said more kind things. Then he called the children up and gave each of them a gold watch engraved with their names.

"You must make a speech now and thank everybody for their kindness," the station master whispered in Peter's ear, putting both hands on Peter's shoulders and gently moving him forwards.

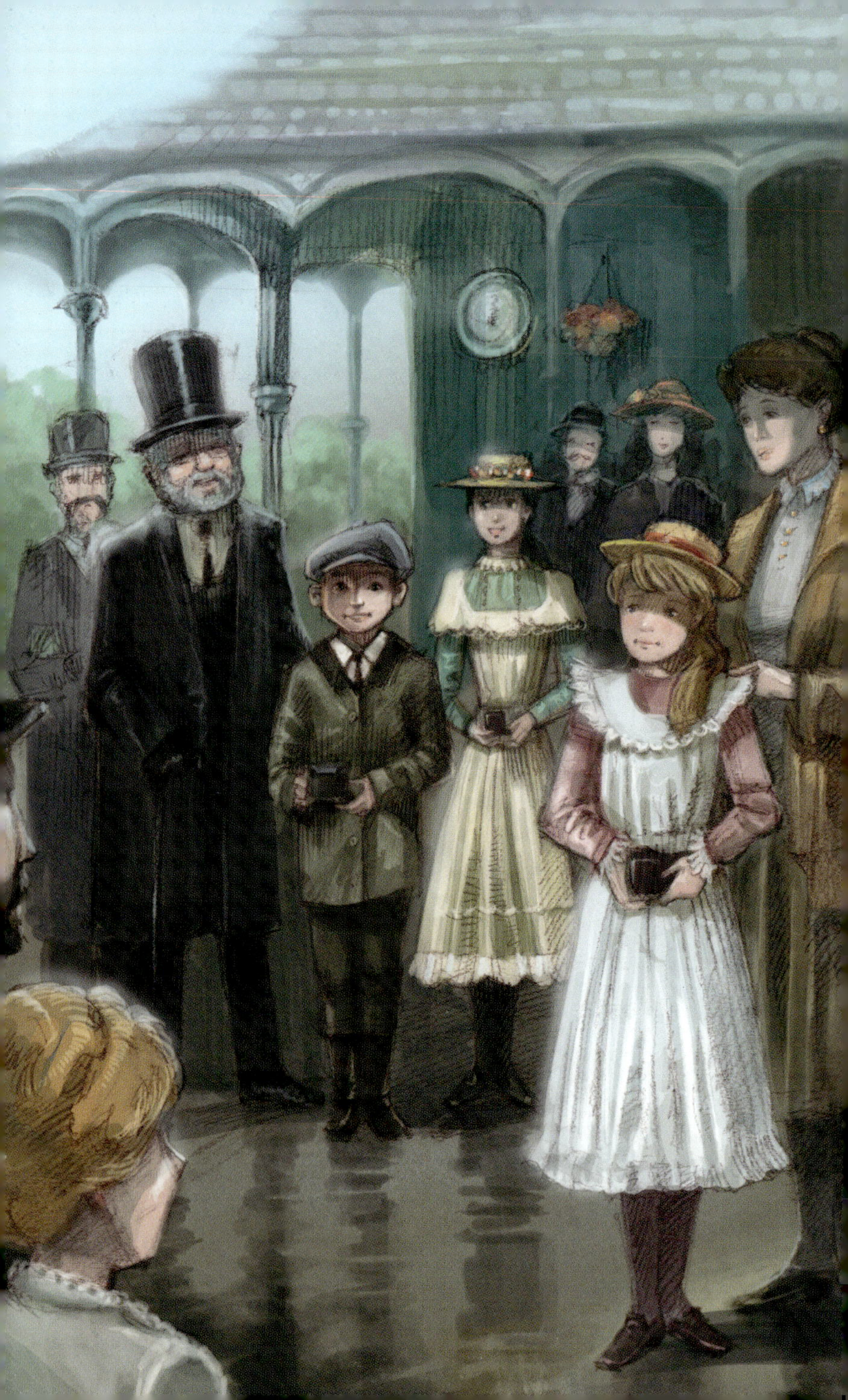

There was a pause and Peter could hear his heart beating in his throat. "Ladies and Gentlemen," he said in a rush. "It's awfully good of you and we shall treasure our watches all our lives. What I mean to say is, thank you all very much."

As soon as it was polite to leave, the children ran back up the hill to the Three Chimneys, with their watches in their hands.

The Russian writer was still living with them. All the Members of Parliament had answered Mother's letters but none of them could tell her where the Russian's wife and children might be. Bobbie had intended to ask their old gentleman to help him but the award ceremony had seemed too public. *I'll write him a letter*, she thought.

Later, she showed the others what she had written.

My dearest old gentleman,

I want to talk to you about a prisoner and captive. If you could get out of the train and go by the next, it would do.

Your friend,
Bobbie

She got the station master to give the letter to the old gentleman, and the next day Bobbie, Peter and Phyllis went down to the station to meet the old gentleman's train.

As the old gentleman stepped from the train, the three children suddenly felt shy.

"It was very good of you to get out," said Bobbie politely.

The old gentleman led the way into the waiting room. "Now, what is this about prisoners and captives?" he asked with a kindly smile.

Bobbie told him about the Russian who had been sent to prison for writing about poor people. "And we want you to try to help us find his wife and child."

"What did you say his name was?" asked the old gentleman.

Bobbie carefully wrote down the Russian writer's name.

"That man?" said the old gentleman, astonished. "Well, I'm glad you came to me about this – very glad indeed. I shouldn't be surprised if I found out something very soon. I know a great many Russians in London and every Russian knows *his* name."

The children walked home feeling that for once they had done something right and good that they could feel proud of.

Just ten days later, they were sitting in the field, watching the 5.15 train steam away from the station along the bottom of the valley. Suddenly they saw someone walking up the track that led to the Three Chimneys.

As the figure drew closer, they saw it was their old gentleman himself, the brass buttons on his waistcoat winking in the sunshine. The children ran to meet him.

"Good news!" he called. "I've found your Russian friend's wife and child."

Bobbie ran ahead and breathlessly panted out the news.

Mother said a few quick French words to the Russian and the Russian sprang up with a cry of love and longing such as Bobbie had never heard. He took Mother's hand and kissed it then he sank down in his chair, covered his face with his hands and sobbed.

Bobbie crept away. She didn't want to see the others just then. But she had fully recovered by the time Peter had run down to the village for buns and cakes.

She and Phyllis got tea ready and took it into the garden, where Mother, the Russian and the old gentleman were talking comfortably together in a mixture of English and French.

After tea, their Russian friend's few belongings were packed and they took him down to the station and waved him off.

Mother said to the old gentleman, "I don't know how to thank you for everything. It has been a real pleasure to meet you at last." The old gentleman bowed and said she was a most charming and gracious lady.

Bobbie, Peter and their mother walked back uphill towards the Three Chimneys, with Phyllis skipping happily beside them.

"How lovely," Phyllis said, "to think of him embracing his long-lost wife. The baby must have grown a lot since he last saw her."

"Yes," said Mother.

"I wonder whether Father will think I've grown," Phyllis said, still skipping. "I have grown, haven't I, Mother?"

"Yes," said Mother. "Yes, you have."

Bobbie saw that Mother was near to tears. "Come on you two. I'll race you to the gate," she said quickly to Peter and Phyllis. She didn't really want to have a race. She just wanted Mother to have a few moments of privacy. So the three children raced on ahead, leaving their mother to walk back up the hill by herself.

CHAPTER EIGHT
The Pride of Perks

"That's a likely little brooch you've got on, Miss," said Perks the porter to Bobbie. "I don't know as I ever see a thing more like a buttercup without it was a buttercup."

"Mother gave it to me for my birthday," Bobbie said.

"Have you had a birthday?" Perks sounded surprised, as though a birthday was something that only happened to a favoured few.

"Yes," said Bobbie. "When's your birthday, Mr Perks?"

The children were having tea with Mr

Perks in the porters' room. They had brought their own cups and some jam turnovers. Mr Perks brewed the tea in a beer can as usual and everyone felt very comfortable together.

"My birthday?" said Perks, tipping dark brown tea into Peter's cup. "I gave up keeping my birthday before you was born."

"But you must have been born sometime, you know," said Phyllis, "even if it was twenty years ago or sixty or seventy."

"Not so long ago as that, Missie," Perks said, grinning. "If you really want to know, it was thirty-two years ago on the fifteenth of this month."

"Then why don't you keep it?" asked Phyllis curiously.

"I've got something else to keep beside birthdays," said Perks darkly.

"What?" said Phyllis.

"The kids and the missus," he said.

"It seems horrid that nobody keeps his birthday," Bobbie said later. "Couldn't we do something?" But none of them could think what they could do.

Next day at breakfast, Mother said, "I've sold another story, so there'll be buns for tea. You can all set off to buy them as soon as they're baked."

The children quickly exchanged glances.

Bobbie said, "Mother, would you mind if we didn't have the buns for tea tonight, but on the fifteenth instead? That's next Thursday."

"I don't mind when you have them," said Mother, "but why?"

"Because it's Perks's birthday," said Bobbie. "He says he doesn't keep his birthday any more because of the kids and the missus."

"We thought we'd make a birthday celebration for him," said Peter. "He's been so decent to us, Mother."

"You could put his name on the buns with pink icing," suggested Mother.

But the children thought that just buns didn't seem like a very grand celebration.

They had a discussion in the hay loft as they dropped stalks of hay into the stables below them.

"We could give him flowers," said Bobbie.

"He's *got* plenty of flowers," said Peter.

"Let's be quiet and think," said Phyllis.

"Hooray! I've got it!" Peter cried, jumping up suddenly.

"What?" said the others.

"There must be lots of people who'd like to give Perks things for his birthday. Let's go 'round the village and ask everybody."

"Mother said we weren't to ask people for things," Bobbie said doubtfully.

"She meant things for *ourselves*, silly, not things for other people!"

So the children made their way to the village to tell everyone about their plan for Perks's birthday.

When they got home Peter carefully wrote down all the things that had been given and the things that had been promised. When they told Mother what they'd been doing she said, "If you're quite sure he won't be offended, I'd like to give him some things, as he's been so kind to you."

The morning of the fifteenth was spent happily buying the buns and watching

Mother put Perks's initials on them in pink icing. While the buns were put into a cool oven to set the sugar, the children went up to the village to collect the other things that people had promised.

Mrs Ramsay at the post office gave them a basket full of gooseberries and a pram for Mrs Perks's baby. "And here's some peppermints for the little ones," she said, beaming.

All the things that had been collected for Perks were packed into the baby's pram, and at half-past three, Peter, Bobbie and Phyllis wheeled it down to the little yellow house where the Perks family lived.

A boy put his head around the door. "Mother's getting changed," he said.

The stairs creaked and Mrs Perks came down buttoning her dress.

"We heard it was Mr Perks's birthday," Peter explained. "We've got some presents for him outside."

When Mrs Perks saw all the presents she burst into tears.

Peter was horrified. "Don't you like it?"

"*Like* it?" she said, drying her eyes. "Why, Perks never had such a birthday, not even when he was a boy."

The children heard the little front gate being unlatched.

"Bless him, he's early!" said Mrs Perks.

"We'll hide in the back kitchen," whispered Bobbie, "and you tell him all about it. And when you've told him we'll come in and shout, 'Many happy returns'."

Peter, Bobbie and Phyllis rushed into the wash house pushing the surprised little Perks children in front of them. There was no time to shut the door, so, without meaning to, they had to listen to what went on in the kitchen.

"Hullo, old woman," they heard Mr Perks say. "What's that pram doing here? And those bundles? And where did all this sweet stuff come from?"

Bobbie gasped. "I forgot to put the labels on any of the things! He'll think it's all from *us* and that we're trying to give him charity or something horrid."

They heard the voice of Mr Perks loud

and angry. "I won't stand it, Nell, I'm telling you straight."

"But it's those children you make such a fuss about," said Mrs Perks, "the children from the Three Chimneys."

"I don't care if it's an angel from heaven," said Perks. "I'm not accepting charity at my time of life, so don't you think it."

"Oh, shut your silly tongue, Bert," said poor Mrs Perks. "They're in the wash house listening to every word you say."

"Then I'll give them something to listen to," said the angry Perks. He took two strides to the wash-house door and flung it open. "Come out and tell me what you mean by it," he demanded. "Have I ever complained to you of being hard-up? Have I?"

Phyllis burst into tears.

"We thought you'd love it," said Bobbie. "We always have things on our birthdays."

"From your own relations, that's different," said Perks.

"Not just our relations," said Bobbie. "Mrs Viney gave me two lovely glass pots and nobody thought it was charity."

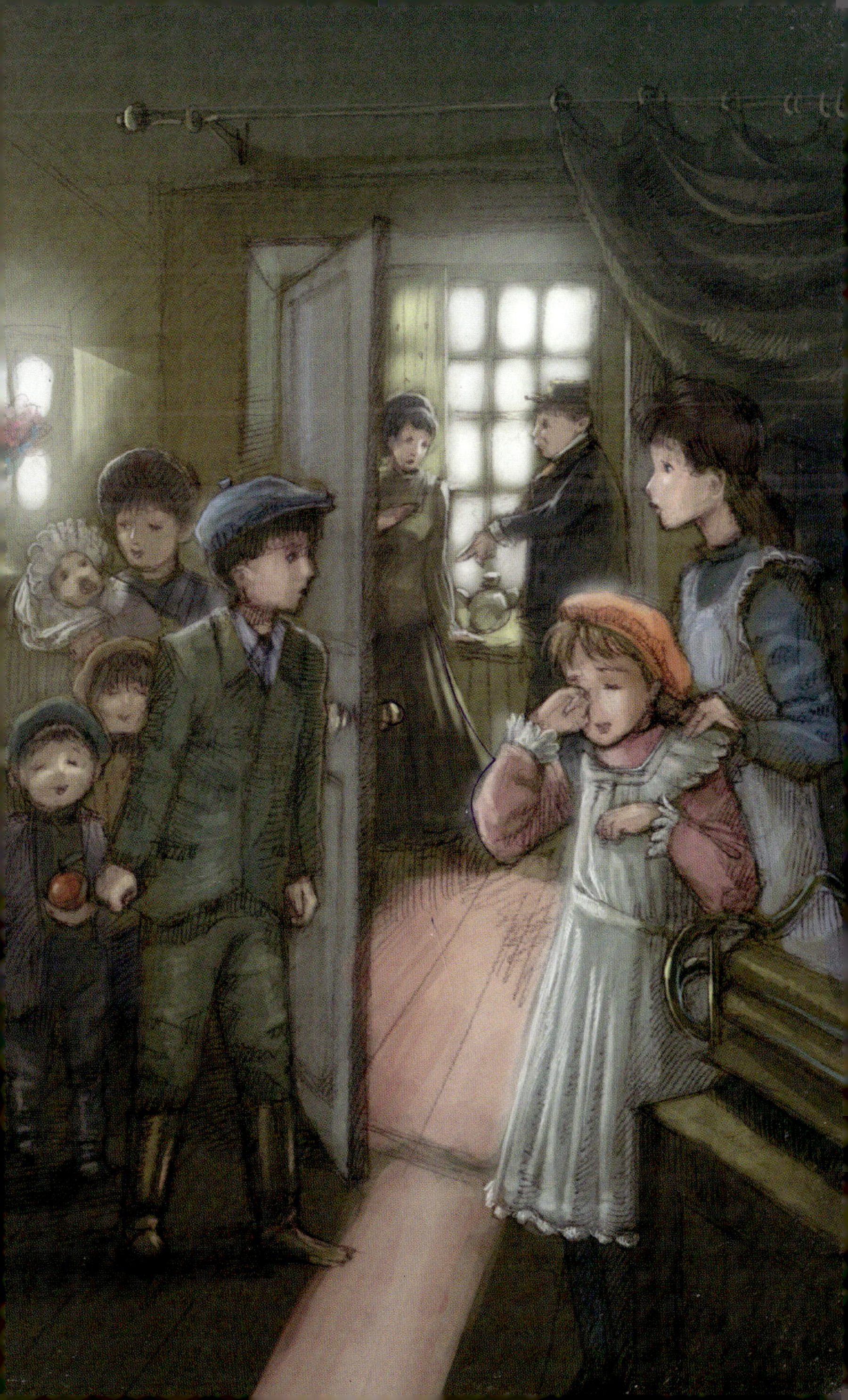

"Glass pots would have been all right," said Perks. "It's all these heaps of things I can't stand."

"They're not all from us," said Peter. "Most of them are from people in the village."

Perks sat down heavily on a chair. "So you've been 'round telling the neighbours we can't make ends meet. Well, you can just take it all back where it came from, and if you don't mind I'd rather not be acquainted with you any longer." And he deliberately turned his back to the children.

"You needn't be friends with us if you don't want," said Bobbie, trying not to cry. "But before we go, do let us show you the labels we wrote to put on the things." She fumbled in her pocket. "I wrote down what everybody said when they gave us them." She had to blink back her tears before she could begin reading.

"Mother's first. Little clothes for Mrs Perks's children," Bobbie read out. "Mother said, 'If you're quite sure Mr Perks won't be offended, I'd like to give him something because he's been so kind to you.'"

"Your Ma's a born lady," said Perks gruffly. "We'll keep the little frocks, Nell."

"The gooseberries and peppermints and the baby's pram are from Mrs Ramsay," said Bobbie. "She said, 'I'd like Mrs Perks to have the pram. It would be a great help for her fine boy.'"

"I can't send the pram back, Bert, and I won't, so don't ask me," said Mrs Perks.

"Then the shovel," Bobbie went on bravely. "Mr James, the blacksmith, made it for you himself. He said, 'You tell Mr Perks it's a pleasure to make a little trifle for a man as is so much respected.'" She hurried through the rest of the labels. "Everybody who gave anything said they liked you and nobody said anything about charity." By this time tears were streaming down Bobbie's face. "I never was so unhappy in all my life," she choked. "I hope you'll forgive us one day." And she fled towards the back door.

"Stop!" said Perks. "Nell, put on the kettle."

"We'll take the things away, if you're

unhappy about them," said Peter.

Perks swung round to face them. "I'm not unhappy," he said. "I don't know as I was ever better pleased! Not with the presents, but the kind respect of our neighbours. That's worth having, eh, Nell?"

"It's *all* worth having," said Mrs Perks. "You've made a fuss about nothing, Bert."

He shook his head. "If a man doesn't respect himself, no one will do it for him."

"Everyone respects you," said Bobbie. "They all said so."

"I *knew* you'd like it when you understood!" Phyllis said, beaming.

"Humph!" said Mr Perks. "You'll stay to tea, I hope?"

"Jolly good little kids, those," said Mr Perks to his wife as they went to bed.

"They're all right," said his wife. "It's *you* I was ashamed of."

"I climbed down as soon as I understood it wasn't charity," he said. "Charity is something I never could abide."

"Oh, *drat* charity," said Mrs Perks

impatiently. "It was friendliness – *that's* what it was – just kindness and friendliness!"

CHAPTER NINE
The Terrible Secret

Every day Mother sat in her room, writing stories to make ends meet. One day, as usual, Bobbie took her up a cup of tea.

Laying down her pen, Mother ran her hands through her hair as if she was going to pull it out.

"Does your head ache?" asked Bobbie.

"Not too much," said Mother. "Bobbie, do you think Peter and Phyllis are forgetting Father?"

"No!" said Bobbie indignantly. "We often talk about him."

"But not to me," said Mother. "Why not?"

"You were so unhappy about Father not being here," said Bobbie. "It made you worse when we talked about him. So we stopped."

"It did hurt to hear you all talking about him as if everything were just the same," Mother admitted. "But it would be *much* more terrible if you were to forget him."

For Mother's sake, Bobbie had tried her best not to wonder what had happened to their father. He was not dead; Mother had said so. And being poor wasn't the trouble. It was something much bigger than just money.

"This trouble," she burst out. "It won't last always, will it?"

Mother put her arms around Bobbie. "No," she promised. "The worst will be over when Father comes home to us."

"I wish we could help you," said Bobbie.

"You do!" said Mother. "You do kind things like putting flowers in my room and cleaning my shoes. And you don't quarrel nearly so much as you used to."

I am so pleased Mother noticed about us not quarrelling, Bobbie thought, and she made a promise to herself that they would keep this up.

Only a few hours later, Bobbie and Peter got into an argument over the garden rake. Bobbie remembered just in time that they weren't supposed to quarrel, but Peter was being so insulting that she just said, "Here, *take* the horrid rake then!" and suddenly let it go.

Peter fell over backwards with a loud shriek. When Mother undid his boots, red blood dripped from his foot onto the ground and there were three red wounds where the teeth of the rake had bitten him.

The doctor told them that Peter would be housebound until his injury healed.

They moved the sofa to the window and from there Peter could see the smoke of the trains winding along the valley. But he could not see the trains.

"I wish I had something to read," said Peter one day. "I've read all our books about fifty times."

Bobbie badly wanted to make amends

for injuring her brother. "Perks has heaps of magazines at the station," she said. "I'll run down and ask him."

She found Perks cleaning lamps. "How's the young gent?" he said.

"Better, thanks, but he's frightfully bored. I came to ask if you'd got any magazines you could lend him."

"I've got some illustrated papers left," he said, "and if he wants to colour in the pictures with his coloured chalks, let him. *I* don't want them! I'll put a bit of paper round them for you." He pulled an old newspaper out from the pile and wrapped it all up like a parcel.

The papers were heavy, and when Bobbie had to wait at the level-crossing while a train went by, she rested the parcel on the top of the gate, idly reading the print on the paper the parcel was wrapped in.

Suddenly she clutched the parcel tighter, bending closer as she read the dreadful words in the newspaper.

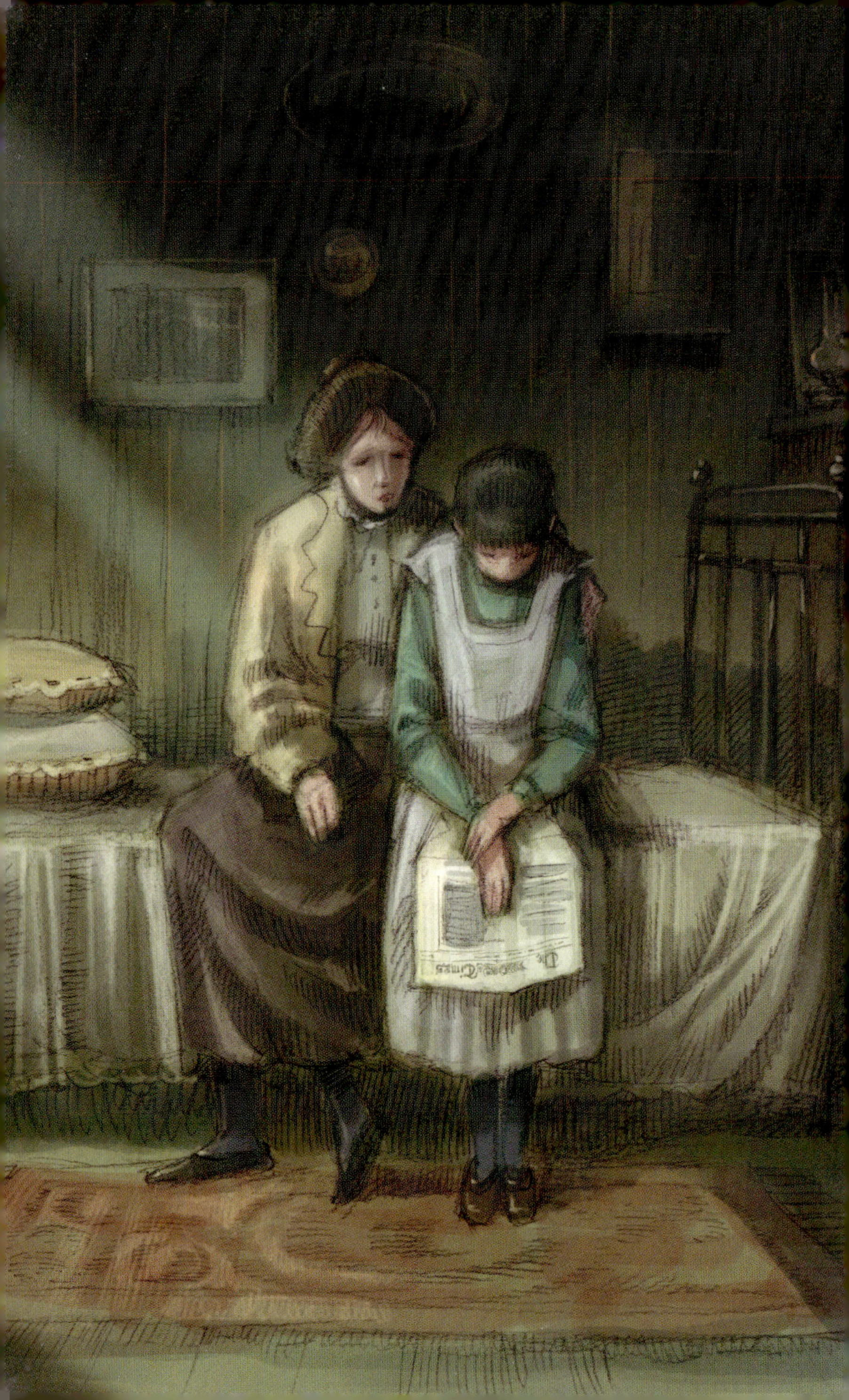

She never remembered how she got home. She went up to her room and locked the door. Sitting on the edge of her bed, she read the chilling words over and over: 'End of the Trial. Verdict. Sentence.'

The name of the man being tried was her father. The verdict was 'Guilty'.

Bobbie went to find her mother in the kitchen. She caught at her hand.

"What is it?" said Mother.

"Come up to my room," said Bobbie, "where nobody can hear us."

Once they were inside Bobbie locked the door. She pulled out the paper from under her mattress and held it out, pointing to Father's name with a finger that shook.

"Oh, Bobbie," said Mother, when she saw what it was. "You don't *believe* it? You don't believe Daddy did it?"

"No!" Bobbie almost shouted.
"Because it's not true, darling. They've shut him up in prison but he's done nothing wrong. We have to think of that and be proud of him and wait."

"Mother, will it make you feel worse if you tell me all about it?" Bobbie asked. "I want to understand."

Mother put her arms around Bobbie and explained that the two strange men who had come to the Red House that night had arrested Father for being a spy. She told Bobbie about the trial and about the evidence – letters found in Father's desk at his office – that convinced the jury that Father was guilty.

"But how did the letters get into his desk?" asked Bobbie.

"Someone must have put them there," said Mother with a sigh.

"But couldn't we explain to someone?"

"No, my dearest. All we can do, you and I and Daddy, is to be brave and patient. We won't talk of this any more, will we, Bobbie?" said Mother. "Wash your face and let's go out into the garden for a bit."

A week later, Bobbie managed to get away alone. And once more she wrote a letter and once more it was to the old gentleman.

My dear friend,

You see what's in this paper? It's not true. Mother says someone put the papers in Father's desk. Can you find out who did the treason and then they would let Father out of prison. Mother told us once to pray for all prisoners and captives and now I know why. Oh, please do help us.

With love,
Your friend, Roberta

She cut the story of her father's trial out of the newspaper and put it in the envelope with her letter. Then she took it down to the station, going out the back way so that the others would not see her.

CHAPTER TEN
The Hound in the Red Jersey

When Bobbie got back, she had some exciting news for Peter and Phyllis.

"Perks says to tell you the boys from the grammar school are having a paper chase. We could take our lunch and go along the cutting and watch. You can see a long way from there."

They set out walking along the track where workmen were clearing up the remains of the landslide with picks and spades and wheelbarrows.

Suddenly a voice panted, "Let me pass

please." The boy had a bag of torn paper under his arm, fastened by a strap.

"He's the hare!" said Phyllis.

Next came the 'hounds', following the white paper trail left by the hare. There were thirty of them. Bobbie, Phyllis and Peter counted them as they climbed down the ladder-like steps. Still following the white blobs of scattered paper, they disappeared into the tunnel.

When the last boy, in a red jersey, vanished into the darkness, the children decided to cut across the top so they could see the hounds come out at the other end of the tunnel.

They were just in time to see the hare coming out from the shadow of the tunnel.

"Now for the hounds!" said Peter.

After a few minutes, tired-looking boys began to emerge from the tunnel. One or two were lagging far behind.

"Now, let's have lunch!" said Phyllis.

"The boy in the red jersey hasn't come out yet," said Peter.

They waited and waited but the boy in the red jersey didn't appear.

"He might have had an accident," said Peter. "We'd better go into the tunnel and see. I'll go first, though, because it was my idea."

Inside the tunnel, stones and gravel slid and shifted under their feet. Slimy trickles of water ran down the walls, which were not red brick but a slimy sickly green.

"I want to go back," said Phyllis. "It'll be pitch dark in a minute."

"Don't be such a cuckoo. I've got some matches and a candle-end," said Peter.

They heard a low humming sound on the railway line.

"It's a train!" said Bobbie.

Just in time, she and Peter dragged Phyllis to the safety of an archway.

With a rush and roar and a dazzling flash of lighted carriage windows, a smell of smoke and blast of hot air, the train hurtled by.

Peter struck a match and lit a candle end with a hand that shook. "Come on," he said.

The three children went on into the deeper darkness of the tunnel. Peter led, holding his candle-end high to light the way. Suddenly he said, "Hullo"– and began to run.

The girls were horrified to see the boy with the red jersey slumped with his back against the wall.

Phyllis shut her eyes. "Is he killed?"

"He's only fainted, silly," said Peter. "We should splash his face with water."

"We've only got milk," said Bobbie.

So they splashed the boy's face with warmish milk.

After a while, he sighed and opened his eyes. Then he tried to move and groaned.

"Do you think you could walk if we helped you?" asked Peter.

He tried and almost fainted with the pain. "I think I've broken my leg," he said.

"I'll stay with him, Peter," said Bobbie bravely. "You and Phyllis go and get help. Take the longest candle-end. But please hurry up because this little bit of candle won't last long!"

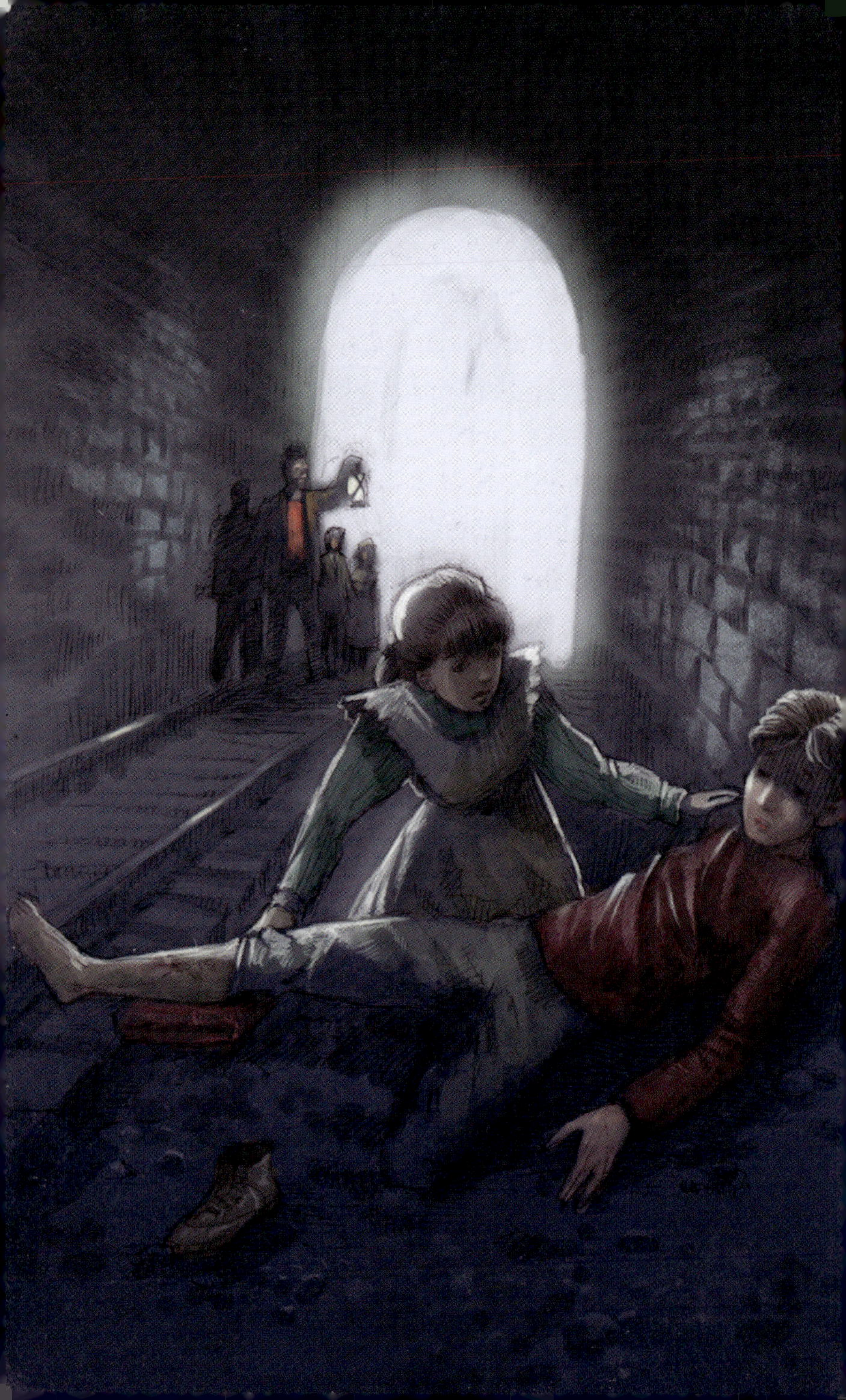

She watched Peter's candle move off, leaving her and the injured boy in the almost pitch darkness. While they waited for help, Bobbie talked to the boy, trying to keep his mind off his pain. He told her that he came from Northumberland and his name was Jim. It was very cold.

At last Phyllis and Peter came back with two strong men and a hurdle covered with horse cloths for a stretcher.

"Bring him up to our house," said Bobbie. "I know Mother would want us to."

Some time later, Mother's work-room door flew open and a breathless Bobbie burst in. She panted out the story of finding the injured boy in the tunnel. "His mother's dead, and his father's in Northumberland. I said they should bring him here, because you always help everybody."

Sighing a little, Mother arrived downstairs just as Jim was carried in, half-fainting. "I'm so sorry to give you all this trouble," he said weakly.

"Now, Jim, let's get you comfortable

before the doctor comes," said Mother, and she kissed him just as if he'd been Peter. "We love having you here, don't we, Bobbie?"

Mother had no chance of doing any writing that day. The doctor came and set Jim's leg. Afterwards, Mother had to send telegrams to Jim's school and to Jim's grandfather who was also Jim's guardian.

"Did you tell Jim's grandfather that Jim can stay with us?" asked Peter hopefully.

"I would love Jim to stay," said Mother, "but I can't nurse him at the same time as doing my writing."

Next morning, after breakfast, a knock came at the door. The children were hard at work cleaning the brass candlesticks in honour of Jim's visit. "That'll be the doctor," said Mother. "I'll go. Shut the kitchen door – you're all too dirty to be seen."

It wasn't the doctor. The children knew by the sound of the voice and the boots going upstairs. "Who can it be?" they kept asking each other.

"Bobbie!" called Mother's voice. They

opened the kitchen door and Mother leaned over the banister. "Jim's grandfather has come. Wash your hands and faces. He wants to see you."

They were still busy with soap and flannels when they heard the voice and the boots come back down the stairs and go into the dining room. They quickly filed in after him, impatient to see this mysterious grandfather. Mother was sitting in the window-seat and in Father's leather-covered armchair sat their old gentleman!

"It's *you*!" said Bobbie, astonished.

"I'm so glad!" said Phyllis. "When I think of all the old gentlemen there are in the world, it might have been anyone!"

"You're not going to take Jim away, are you?" asked Peter, anxiously.

The old gentleman shook his head. "Your mother has kindly agreed to have him here."

"But what about her writing?" said Peter before he could stop himself. "There won't be anything for him to eat here if Mother doesn't write."

The old gentleman smiled. "Your mother is going to give up writing for a while and nurse my grandson, and I will send a housemaid and a cook to help her out until Jim's well."

"When will Mother go on writing again?" asked Peter.

The old gentleman gave Bobbie a swift glance. "Maybe something wonderful will happen and she won't have to."

"I love my writing," said Mother very quickly.

"I know," said the old gentleman. "But sometimes wonderful things do happen, don't they, and we live most of our lives in hope of them. May I come back to see Jim?" he asked.

"Of course," said Mother.

"Dear me, where's my hat?" said the old gentleman. "Will Bobbie come with me to the gate?"

At the gate he stopped and said quietly, "I got your letter, you dear child, but it wasn't needed. I read about your father's case and ever since I met you, I've been trying to find things out."

"You don't think Father did it, do you?" said Bobbie tearfully.

"My dear, I'm perfectly *certain* he didn't."

And for the very first time since Father was arrested, a small spark of hope entered Bobbie's heart, staying with her for the days that followed.

CHAPTER ELEVEN
Bobbie Meets the Train

Life at the Three Chimneys was never quite the same again after the old gentleman came to visit his grandson. Now that Mother had help in the house she had time to spend with her children again. She even wrote a funny rhyming poem for Jim who was well enough now to sit up and play chess and dominoes with them.

They hardly seemed to be railway children at all in those days and, as time went on, all three children began to feel strangely restless.

"I wonder if the railway misses us?" Phyllis said one morning. "We never go to see it now."

Bobbie agreed. "The thing I don't like is our having stopped waving to the 9.15 and sending our love to Father."

Peter glanced at his watch. "If we hurry, we could go and wave to it now."

They ran and were just in time to wave their handkerchiefs to the 9.15.

"Take our love to Father!" they cried.

The old gentleman waved his newspaper. There was nothing odd about this for he always waved. What was really remarkable was that from every window passengers wildly waved their newspapers.

The train swept by with a roar and the children were left looking at each other.

"Did you think the old gentleman's wave seemed different to usual?" asked Bobbie. "I thought he was trying to explain something with his newspaper."

"Explain what?" said Peter.

"I don't know," said Bobbie. "But I feel awfully strange. It's as if something is about to happen."

Bobbie went on feeling strange all through lessons. "Mother, will you let me off lessons today?" she asked abruptly.

"You don't feel ill, do you?" asked Mother.

"I don't know," Bobbie answered. "I feel as if I want to be quite alone, by myself."

She went into the garden, but the hollyhocks and the late summer roses all seemed to be waiting for something to happen.

I'll go down to the station and see Perks, she decided.

On the way she passed Mrs Ramsay from the post office. She surprised Bobbie by stopping to give her a kiss and a hug. "God bless you, love," she said beaming.

The blacksmith went by, grinning broadly and waving his newspaper. "Good morning, Miss. I wish you joy, that I do!"

Bobbie's heart quickened. "Something is going to happen," she whispered. "Everyone is so odd, like people in dreams."

At the station, Perks was nowhere to be seen, but the station master hurried up to Bobbie smiling and warmly shook her hand.

"The 11.45's a bit late," he said apologetically, then disappeared into his office without explanation.

Even the station cat came to rub herself, purring, against Bobbie's stockings.

"How kind everybody is today," said Bobbie, "even you, Puss!"

Perks didn't appear until the 11.45 was signalled and like everyone else he had a newspaper under his arm. "God bless you, my dear," he said. "I don't think I was ever so glad of anything in all my born days." And with that he kissed Bobbie first on one cheek and then on the other. "You ain't offended are you?" he asked anxiously. "I ain't took a liberty? On a day like this, you know?"

"No, no," said Bobbie, bewildered. "Of course not, but on a day like *what*, Mr Perks?"

"Didn't I tell you? I saw it in the paper!"

"Saw what in the paper?" said Bobbie, but the 11.45 was steaming in. Perks had to rush away, leaving Bobbie alone with just the station cat for company.

Only three people got out of the train: a countryman with chickens, a woman carrying a tin box and three brown-paper parcels – and the third …

"*Oh! My daddy, my daddy!*" Bobbie screamed in amazement.

She almost flew down the platform towards a tall, pale man.

Hearing her scream, people put their heads out of the train windows and saw Bobbie hurl herself at her father, as his arms went tightly aound her.

"I knew something wonderful was going to happen," Bobbie said, walking home with Father and clinging tightly to his hand. "But I didn't know it was going to be you."

"Didn't Mother get my letter?" asked her father.

"We didn't get any letters today," said Bobbie. "Oh, Daddy, it *is* really you, isn't it?"

"You go in by yourself, Bobbie," said Father when they had reached the house. "Tell Mother quite quietly that everything is all right. They've caught the man who did it.

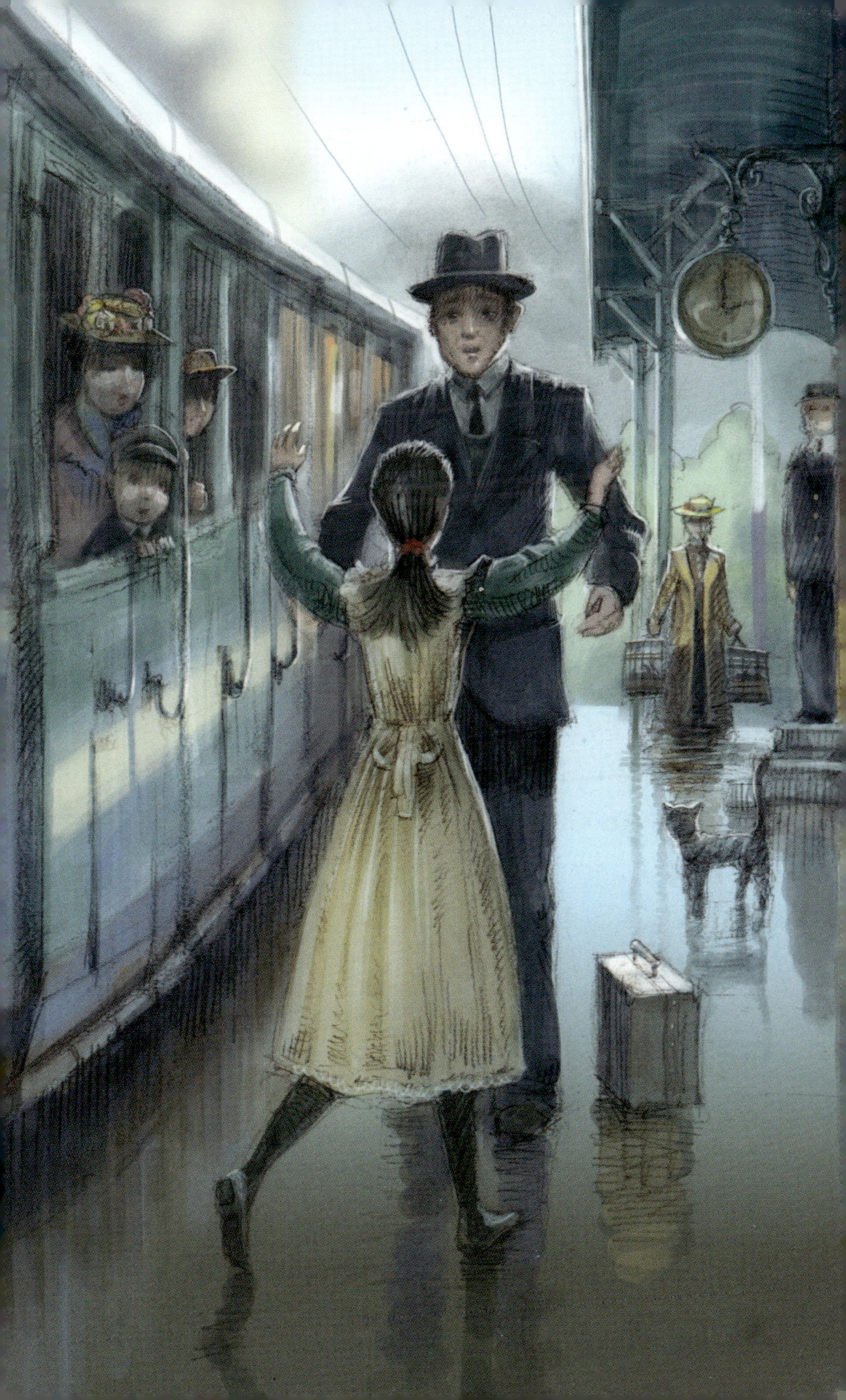

Everyone knows now that it wasn't me."

And so Bobbie went inside to tell their mother that the long parting was over. Father had come home to them at last.

Father waited outside among the late summer flowers, but his eyes kept turning towards the house.

Eventually a door opened and Bobbie called. "Come in, Daddy. Come in!"

Softly closing the door of the cottage, Bobbie, Phyllis and Peter slipped out into the flowering fields, leaving their parents alone together. They understood that, just now, neither they nor anyone else was needed there with them.